Sofia the First

Ages 5–6

DISNEY
LEARNING

WPK.

Add

LEARNING WORKBOOK

Scholastic Children's Books
Euston House,
24 Eversholt Street,
London NW1 1DB, UK

A division of Scholastic Ltd
London • New York • Toronto • Sydney • Auckland
Mexico City • New Delhi • Hong Kong

This book was first published in Australia in 2014 by Scholastic Australia.
Published in the UK by Scholastic Ltd in 2015.

ISBN 978 1 4071 6306 2

Printed in Italy

2 4 6 8 10 9 7 5 3 1

Papers used by Scholastic Children's Books are made from woods grown in sustainable forests.

Welcome to the Disney Learning Programme!

Children learn best when they are having fun! The **Disney Learning Workbooks** are an engaging way for your child to explore basic maths, along with fun characters from the wonderful world of Disney.

The **Disney Learning Workbooks** are carefully levelled to present new challenges to developing learners. Designed to support the National Curriculum for Maths at Key Stage 1, they offer your child the opportunity to practise skills learned at school and to consolidate their learning in a relaxed home setting with support from you. With stickers, games, speed challenges and more, your child will have fun developing their basic addition skills!

The ability to recall maths facts quickly fosters number confidence. This book uses a number of visual images and strategies to help children learn basic addition facts. As children become more proficient in recalling maths facts, they won't need to stop and count any more. Instead, they can devote more mental energy to solving complex maths problems quickly and confidently.

Threaded through the book you will also find a 'Let's Read' story, featuring the characters from Disney's **Sofia the First** for you to enjoy sharing with your child. Reading for pleasure and enjoying books together are fundamental parts of learning. Keep sessions fun and short. Your child may wish to work independently on some of the activities, or you may enjoy doing them together – either way is fine.

Have fun with the Disney Learning programme!

Developed in conjunction with Nicola Spencer, Maths Specialist Teacher

Let's Learn Addition Facts

What is 5 plus 3? How many other ways can you think of to make 8? This book will give you lots of practice making and adding numbers in different ways. You'll find stickers, games and lots more to help you become a terrific problem solver.

You can do it! Let's begin!

Addition
Addition is when you join two numbers or groups together to find out how many there are in total. We use the + sign to add.

1 bird + 2 more birds makes 3 birds in total.

Number Sentences

It doesn't matter which order you add numbers in because you will still get the same total. Look at the number sentences below.

$$5 + 3 = \boxed{8}$$

$$3 + 5 = \boxed{8}$$

Hint

If you know that $4 + 6 = 10$ then you know that $6 + 4 = 10$.

Number Line

A number line can help you solve addition problems. For $3 + 2$, start at 3, then count on 2. Stop at 5.

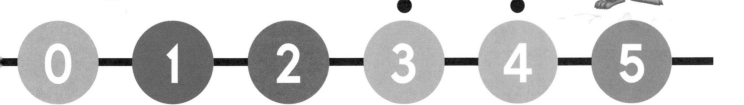

One beautiful day in Enchancia, three grand coaches land at the royal picnic grounds. They belong to three royal families from three different kingdoms: Wei-Ling, Khaldoun and Enchancia.

'Each kingdom at the picnic competes in the Tri-Kingdom games. The winning kingdom will receive the Golden Chalice,' Amber explains to Sofia. 'This year, you and James will play for Enchancia!'

Sofia greets the princesses from the other families. Princess Jun of Wei-Ling is sweet and funny. Princess Maya of Khaldoun has a friendly grin and a sporty look. Sofia can't wait to get to know them better.

Sofia and James change their clothes. Then Sofia meets Maya's brother, Prince Khalid, and Jun's brother, Prince Jin. Baileywick calls for the first game to start – the Flying Horseshoe Toss.

'Be careful,' says James. 'These flying horseshoes like to swoop off course!'

Let's Count to 20

Use the stickers to fill in the missing numbers.

1	2	3	4	5
6	7	8	9	10
11	12	13	14	15
16	17	18	19	20

Use the stickers to fill in the missing numbers.

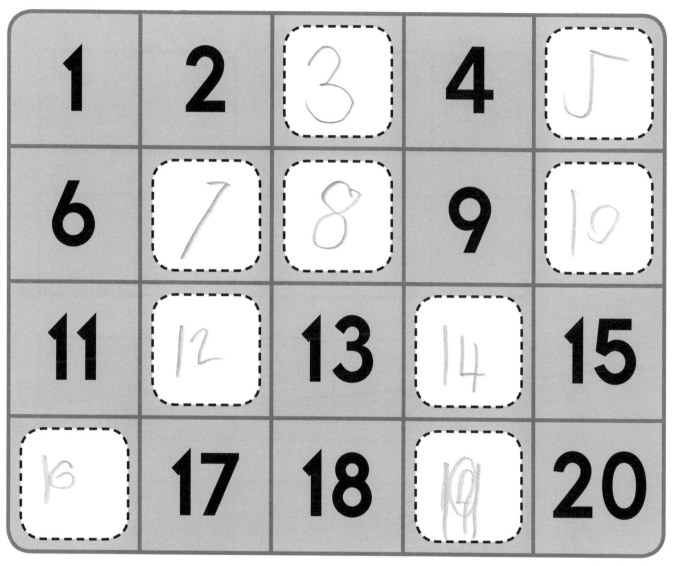

1	2	3	4	5
6	7	8	9	10
11	12	13	14	15
16	17	18	19	20

Let's Make Number Sets

Use the royal coach stickers to show how many.
The first one is done for you.

1

2

3

4

5

Sofia counts royal coaches. Draw more coaches to make 10 in total. Write the number in the number sentence.

3

3 + ☐ = 10

6

6 + ☐ = 10

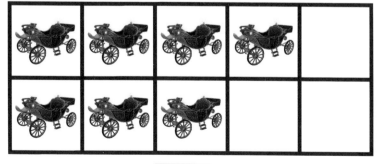

7

7 + ☐ = 10

Let's Show Different Ways to Make Numbers

Show different ways to make 4, 5, 6 and 7. Colour the hats blue and pink. The first one is done for you. Read the number sentences out loud.

4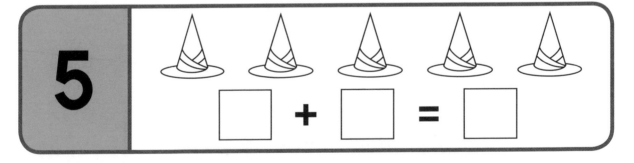

2 + 2 = 4

4

☐ + ☐ = ☐

5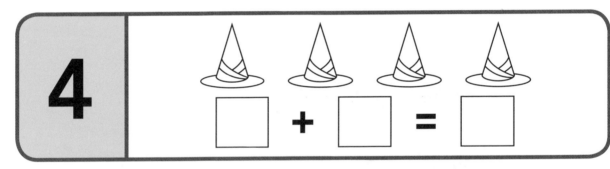

☐ + ☐ = ☐

5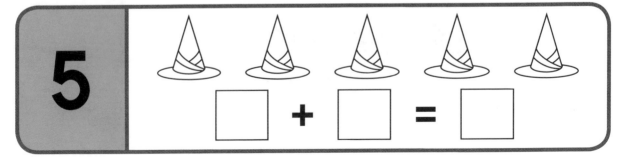

☐ + ☐ = ☐

6

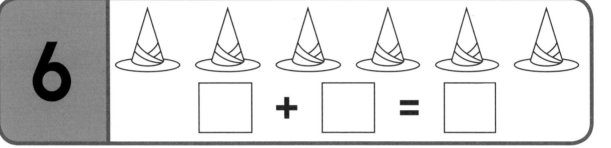

☐ + ☐ = ☐

6

☐ + ☐ = ☐

7

☐ + ☐ = ☐

7

☐ + ☐ = ☐

Let's Show Different Ways to Make Numbers

Show different ways to make 8, 9 and 10.
Colour the crowns blue and yellow.
The first one is done for you.

| 8 | 4 + 4 = 8 |

| 8 | ☐ + ☐ = ☐ |

| 9 | ☐ + ☐ = ☐ |

| 9 | ☐ + ☐ = ☐ |

10 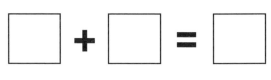 $\boxed{} + \boxed{} = \boxed{}$

10 $\boxed{} + \boxed{} = \boxed{}$

10 $\boxed{} + \boxed{} = \boxed{}$

10  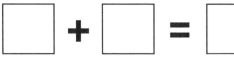 $\boxed{} + \boxed{} = \boxed{}$

Let's Find the Total

Find the stickers that show how many birds there are in total. Fill in the missing numbers. The first one is done for you.

| 1 | add | 2 | makes | 3 | . |

| ☐ | add | ☐ | makes | ☐ | . |

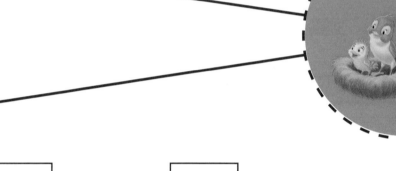

The birds are singing! Find the stickers that show
how many musical notes there are in total.
Fill in the missing numbers.

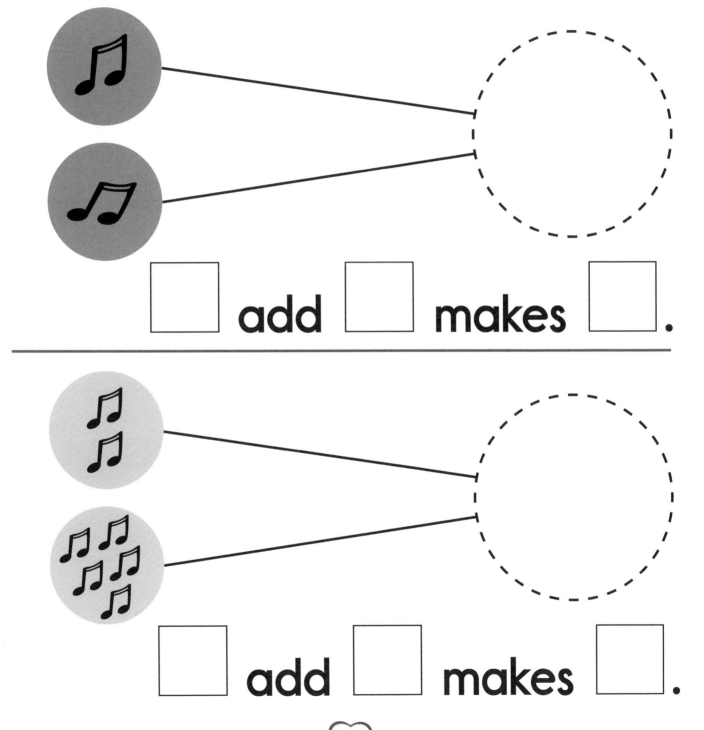

☐ add ☐ makes ☐.

☐ add ☐ makes ☐.

Let's Add 1

Draw 1 more.
Count how many. Write how many in total.
The first one is done for you.

 add 1 more 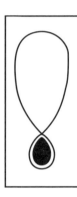 makes .

 add 1 more  makes .

 add 1 more  makes .

Draw 2 more.
Count how many. Write how many in total.

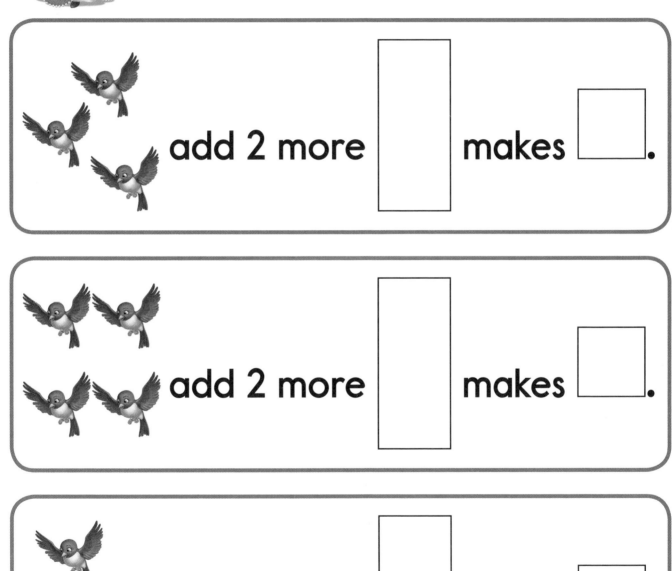

add 2 more [   ] makes [   ].

add 2 more [   ] makes [   ].

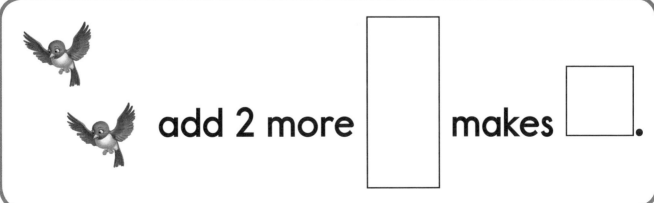

add 2 more [   ] makes [   ].

Let's Add Zero

Count the number of flowers. Add zero and write the total number of flowers. The first one is done for you. **Hint:** Adding zero means that nothing is added.

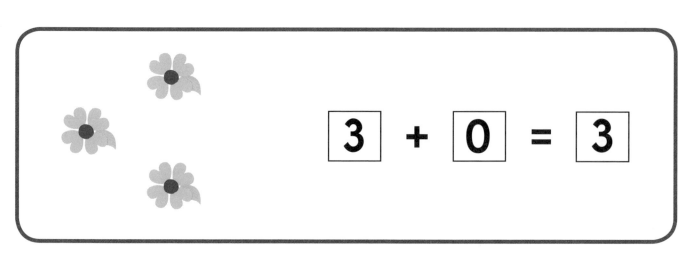

$$3 + 0 = 3$$

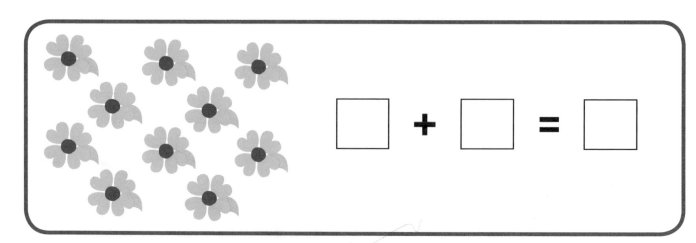

$$\boxed{} + \boxed{} = \boxed{}$$

$$\boxed{} + \boxed{} = \boxed{}$$

Help Sofia compete in the Flying Horseshoe Toss!

First Sofia throws 5 horseshoes.

Then Sofia throws 8 horseshoes.

How many horseshoes has Sofia thrown in total?

Write the number sentence.

☐ + ☐ = ☐

Let's Find the Totals

Add the numbers. Write the answers.
The first one is done for you.

$5 + 3 =$ _8_

$4 + 3 =$ ___

$3 + 1 =$ ___

$7 + 2 =$ ___

Add the numbers.
Write the answers.

5 + 2 = ___

6 + 3 = ___

7 + 1 = ___

4 + 2 = ___

Let's Tell Maths Stories

Complete the maths stories by filling in the gaps.

Amber has _____ s.

She keeps them in her treasure box.

Sofia has _____ s.

She keeps them under her pillow.

Draw the number of jewels that Amber and Sofia each have.

Amber	Sofia

How many jewels do they have altogether?

Write the number sentence and work out the total.

☐ + ☐ = ☐

Clover and Whatnaught
love apples.

Clover has _____ s.
James gave them to him.

Whatnaught finds _____ more apples.

Draw the number of apples that Clover and
Whatnaught each have.

Whatnaught	Clover

How many apples do they have altogether?

Write the number sentence.

 + =

Let's Make Doubles

Add the numbers to double them.
Write the answers.

1 + 1 = ___

2 + 2 = ___

3 + 3 = ___

4 + 4 = ___

5 + 5 = ___

6 + 6 = ___

7 + 7 = ___

8 + 8 = ___

9 + 9 = ___

10 + 10 = ___

Let's Write Number Sentences

Sofia borrows books from the library.
Write the number sentence shown by the two groups.
Find and write the total. The first one is done for you.

6 + 2 = 8

___ + ___ = ___

___ + ___ = ___

James picks apples from the orchard. Write the number sentence shown by the two groups. Find and write the total.

___ + ___ = ___

___ + ___ = ___

___ + ___ = ___

Let's Find the Totals

Add the numbers and write the answers.
Colour the boxes purple
if the answer is 4 or 8.
The first one is done for you.

3 + 1 = __4__	5 + 1 = ___	5 + 3 = ___	6 + 1 = ___
6 + 0 = ___	1 + 3 = ___	3 + 4 = ___	2 + 2 = ___
4 + 4 = ___	4 + 3 = ___	3 + 5 = ___	5 + 2 = ___
3 + 2 = ___	7 + 1 = ___	4 + 1 = ___	8 + 0 = ___

Add the numbers. Write the totals.
Cross out the characters that match the totals.
The last one left is the winner!

| 4 + 3 = ___ | 3 + 1 = ___ | 7 + 2 = ___ |
| 6 + 4 = ___ | 3 + 2 = ___ | 5 + 3 = ___ |

The winner is number ___ !

Sofia and James are the best at the Flying Horseshoe Toss. 'Enchancia wins!' James cheers.

'Nice one,' says Jin.

Next is the Golden Egg on a Silver Spoon race. When Baileywick says, 'Go,' the children race onto the course, balancing their eggs.

SPLAT! SPLAT! Jin and Khalid drop their eggs within moments.

Then Sofia loses her egg – SPLAT! James and Maya keep going. At the last second, Maya wins!

James is angry. He throws down his egg. SPLAT!
'I should have won,' he complains. The other kids frown.

Sofia pulls James aside. 'It is more fun when everyone is a good sport,' she reminds him. 'No one will play if you brag when you win and get angry when you lose.'

James realises Sofia is right. He goes back to the other kids. 'You were the fastest and the steadiest,' he tells Maya. 'It was close, but you deserved to win!'

Speed Challenge

Solve the calculations.
Record your time and the number of correct answers.
On your marks, get set, go!

1 + 1 = ___	6 + 3 = ___	2 + 1 = ___	5 + 3 = ___
2 + 2 = ___	3 + 3 = ___	8 + 0 = ___	3 + 2 = ___
4 + 2 = ___	5 + 2 = ___	5 + 1 = ___	6 + 1 = ___
9 + 1 = ___	6 + 2 = ___	7 + 1 = ___	8 + 2 = ___
4 + 3 = ___	5 + 5 = ___		

Time to Complete: _____

Total Answers: _____

Total Correct: _____

9 + 0 = ___	5 + 1 = ___	6 + 3 = ___	4 + 4 = ___
4 + 1 = ___	8 + 1 = ___	9 + 1 = ___	3 + 2 = ___
5 + 2 = ___	7 + 3 = ___	5 + 3 = ___	2 + 1 = ___
8 + 2 = ___	2 + 7 = ___	2 + 2 = ___	6 + 6 = ___
4 + 2 = ___	3 + 3 = ___		

Time to Complete: _____

Total Answers: _____

Total Correct: _____

Let's Count

Jewels sparkle and shine! Count the jewels.
Write the total. The first one is done for you.

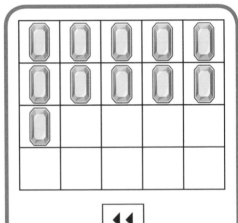

11

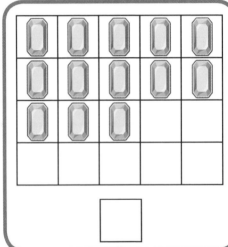

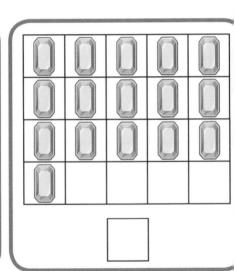

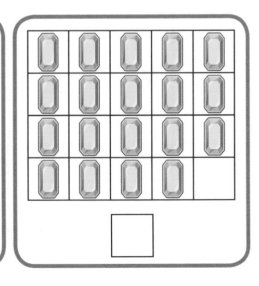

Count the teacups. Write the total.

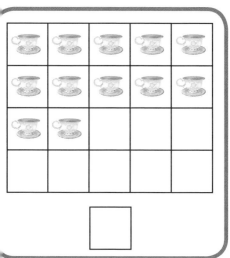

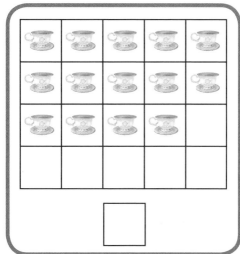

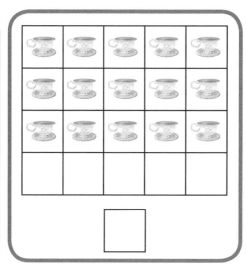

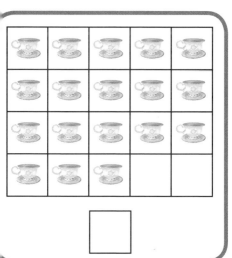

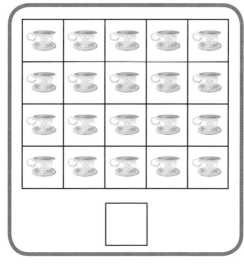

Let's Show Ways to Make 5

Look at the flowers.
Use dots to show different ways 5 flowers can go in 2 vases.
The first one is done for you.

Vase 1	Vase 2	Total
● ● ●	● ●	5
		5
		5
		5

Amber has tapestries.
Use dots to show different ways 9 tapestries can go in 2 rooms.
The first one is done for you.

Room 1	Room 2	Total
● ● ● ● ● ● ● ●	●	9
		9
		9
		9

Find the totals by counting on from the larger number. Write the answer.

$9 + 6 = \underline{15}$

$6 + 5 = \underline{}$

$9 + 3 = \underline{}$

$12 + 8 = \underline{}$

$8 + 9 = \underline{}$

14 + 5 = ____

9 + 9 = ____

9 + 4 = ____

7 + 7 = ____

10 + 6 = ____

Count On With a Number Line

Use the number line. Count on to add.
Write the total. The first one is done for you.

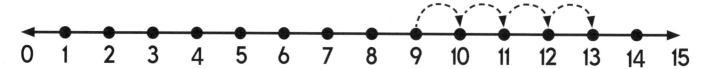

$$9 + 4 = \boxed{13}$$

$$8 + 3 = \boxed{}$$

$$9 + 3 = \boxed{}$$

$$7 + 5 = \boxed{}$$

0　1　2　3　4　5　6　7　8　9　10　11　12　13　14　15

$$8 + 6 = \boxed{}$$

$$9 + 5 = \boxed{}$$

$$8 + 7 = \boxed{}$$

$$9 + 6 = \boxed{}$$

$$7 + 7 = \boxed{}$$

Let's Write Number Sentences

Write the number sentence.
The first one is done for you.

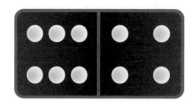

6 + 4 = <u>10</u>

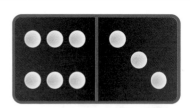

___ + ___ = ___

___ + ___ = ___

___ + ___ = ___

___ + ___ = ___

Draw the missing dots. Write the number sentence.
The first one is done for you.

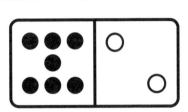

7 + <u>2</u> = 9

6 + __ = 7

5 + __ = 8

__ + __ = 10

__ + __ = 10

Let's Add

Add the numbers. Write the totals.
Colour the boxes that have a total of 15.
The first one is done for you.

9 + 6 = 15	7 + 6 =	8 + 7 =	6 + 5 =
8 + 4 =	9 + 6 =	7 + 4 =	8 + 7 =
9 + 6 =	6 + 4 =	8 + 7 =	7 + 7 =
6 + 3 =	6 + 9 =	9 + 3 =	7 + 8 =
9 + 6 =	8 + 6 =	7 + 8 =	7 + 5 =

Let's Add

Add the numbers. Write the totals.
Colour the boxes that have a total of 18.
The first one is done for you.

11 + 7 = 18	16 + 0 =	11 + 9 =	7 + 11 =
9 + 5 =	9 + 9 =	12 + 5 =	5 + 12 =
6 + 4 =	8 + 7 =	8 + 8 =	0 + 15 =
6 + 6 =	3 + 9 =	13 + 7 =	7 + 7 =
10 + 9 =	10 + 8 =	18 + 0 =	6 + 8 =

Let's Look at a Graph

Look at the graph.
Then answer the questions below.

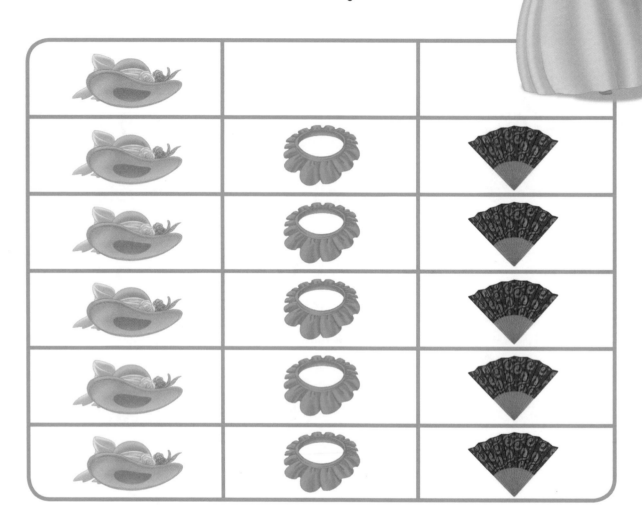

How many s? ____

How many more s than s are there? ____

How many s and s are there
in total? ____

Add across the grid.
Use your stickers to fill in the missing numbers.

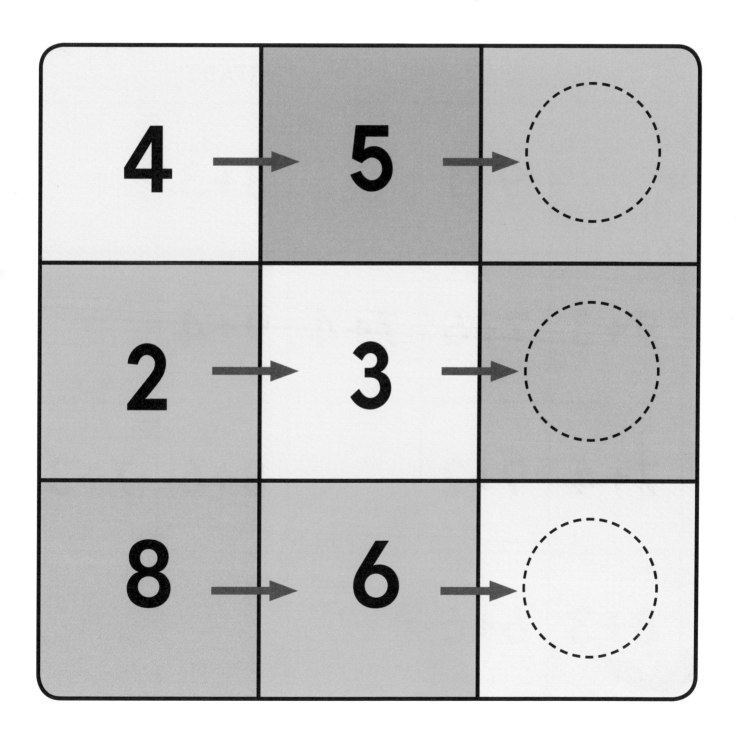

Let's Help the Princesses

Help the princesses get through the maze to the finish line. Colour the squares that have a total of either 11 or 13.

START

	9+1		8+3	
9+3	7+6	7+4	9+4	
7+4	9+2		8+6	7+3
8+3	6+6			

FINISH

Add the numbers. Find the totals.
Cross out the princes and princesses that match the totals.
The person left is the winner!

8 + 5 = ___	7 + 7 = ___	9 + 3 = ___
9 + 2 = ___	6 + 3 = ___	8 + 7 = ___

The winner is number ___ !

Now the adults will compete. They are all making jokes, laughing and having fun. They don't seem to care who is winning or losing. Sofia sees King Roland and Queen Miranda applaud for their friends, the rulers of Wei-Ling.

James comes over to join Sofia. They watch the adults play Bewitching Bowling. James sees his dad mess up his turn – and laugh.

'Oh well,' King Roland says. 'Better luck next time, I hope!'

'Thank you for reminding me of the real reason why we play the Royal Games,' James says to Sofia.

'No problem,' Sofia says to James. 'I just want to make sure that we all have a great picnic and that the kids from the other kingdoms enjoy themselves, too.'

'I'm still glad that we won the Horseshoe Toss,' admits James. 'But I won't mind if one of the other teams takes home the Tri-Kingdom Chalice.'

Speed Challenge

Solve the calculations.
Record your time and the number
of correct answers.
On your marks, get set, go!

6 + 5 = ___	7 + 5 = ___	6 + 6 = ___	8 + 6 = ___
9 + 5 = ___	8 + 4 = ___	7 + 7 = ___	9 + 3 = ___
9 + 4 = ___	7 + 6 = ___	9 + 6 = ___	8 + 5 = ___
9 + 2 = ___	0 + 7 = ___	8 + 7 = ___	8 + 3 = ___
7 + 3 = ___	6 + 4 = ___		

Time to Complete: _____

Total Answers: _____

Total Correct: _____

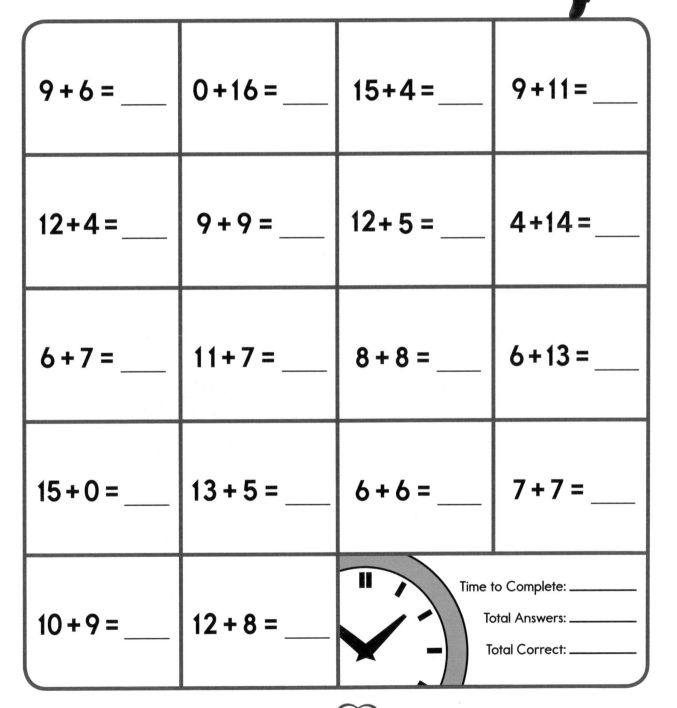

9 + 6 = ___   0 + 16 = ___   15 + 4 = ___   9 + 11 = ___

12 + 4 = ___   9 + 9 = ___   12 + 5 = ___   4 + 14 = ___

6 + 7 = ___   11 + 7 = ___   8 + 8 = ___   6 + 13 = ___

15 + 0 = ___   13 + 5 = ___   6 + 6 = ___   7 + 7 = ___

10 + 9 = ___   12 + 8 = ___

Time to Complete: ___

Total Answers: ___

Total Correct: ___

At the end of the day, Sofia and James get changed back into their formal clothes while Baileywick adds up the scores. When they return, the final results are announced.

'The winner of the Tri-Kingdom Chalice is the Kingdom of Khaldoun!'

Sofia is happy to see that nobody cheers louder than James. The King and Queen of Enchancia come to join them. 'Congratulations, James and Sofia,' says their dad. 'We're proud to see you are both good sports!'

'Would you do the honour of presenting the Golden Chalice to Maya and Khalid?' asks Queen Miranda.

'We'd love to!' replies Sofia.

'Great!' exclaims James.

Maya and Khalid are thrilled to receive the Chalice.

'Maybe we'll win next year,' Sofia says to James. 'Shall we promise to be teammates again?'

He grins and shakes her hand. 'It's a deal!'

Royal Games

Start

VICTORY

VICTORY

VICTORY

Victory Cards

VICTORY

Move ahead 2 spaces

Addition Cards

Move ahead 3 spaces

VICTORY

Move ahead 1 space

VICTORY

VICTORY

© Disney

Royal Games
For 2-4 players

How to Set Up the Game

- Carefully cut out the game pieces found on page 61, following the pink lines.

- Fold each game piece in half on the blue line so it stands upright.

- Carefully cut out each of the addition cards on pages 63 and 65. Mix them up and place them in a pile facedown on the spot marked ADDITION CARDS on the game board.

- Carefully cut out each of the 16 victory cards found on pages 61 and 63 and place them in a pile on the spot marked VICTORY CARDS on the game board.

- Each player chooses a game piece and places his or her game piece on the START space.

- Decide which player will go first.

- Play proceeds in a clockwise direction until there is a winner.

Let's Play Royal Games!

- A player draws a card from the ADDITION CARDS pile and works out the answer. They could use a number line or counting objects to help them.

  - If the answer given is correct, that player moves ahead the number of spaces indicated on the card. Place the used card face up in the centre. It is now the next player's turn.

  - If the answer is incorrect (see Answers on page 61), the player remains on the same space. Place the used card face up in the centre. It is now the next player's turn.

- When the ADDITION CARDS pile is used up, simply mix up the cards again and return them to the ADDITION CARDS pile.

- Each time a player lands on a victory space, they receive one VICTORY CARD.

- The first player to collect four VICTORY CARDS is the winner!

Change the Game!

- You could make some new ADDITION CARDS with different addition calculations.

Answers:

1 + 1 = 2	7 + 1 = 8
2 + 1 = 3	7 + 2 = 9
3 + 1 = 4	7 + 3 = 10
3 + 2 = 5	7 + 4 = 11
3 + 3 = 6	7 + 5 = 12
4 + 2 = 6	7 + 6 = 13
4 + 3 = 7	7 + 7 = 14
4 + 4 = 8	8 + 2 = 10
5 + 1 = 6	8 + 3 = 11
5 + 2 = 7	8 + 4 = 12
5 + 3 = 8	8 + 5 = 13
5 + 4 = 9	8 + 6 = 14
5 + 5 = 10	8 + 7 = 15
6 + 1 = 7	9 + 2 = 11
6 + 2 = 8	9 + 3 = 12
6 + 3 = 9	9 + 4 = 13
6 + 4 = 10	9 + 5 = 14
6 + 5 = 11	9 + 6 = 15

© Disney

Game pieces for Royal Games. ↑

Victory Cards for Royal Games. →

↓

© Disney

Victory Card

Victory Card

Victory Card

Victory Card

Victory Card

Victory Card

Victory Card

Victory Card

Victory Card

Victory Card

1 + 1 Move 1 space	**2 + 1** Move 1 space	**3 + 1** Move 1 space
3 + 2 Move 2 spaces	**3 + 3** Move 2 spaces	**4 + 2** Move 2 spaces
4 + 3 Move 2 spaces	**4 + 4** Move 2 spaces	**5 + 1** Move 2 spaces
5 + 2 Move 3 spaces	**5 + 3** Move 3 spaces	**5 + 4** Move 3 spaces
5 + 5 Move 3 spaces	**6 + 1** Move 3 spaces	**6 + 2** Move 3 spaces

Victory Card	Victory Card	Victory Card
Victory Card	Victory Card	Victory Card
Addition Card	Addition Card	Addition Card
Addition Card	Addition Card	Addition Card
Addition Card	Addition Card	Addition Card
Addition Card	Addition Card	Addition Card
Addition Card	Addition Card	Addition Card

6 + 3	6 + 4	6 + 5
Move 3 spaces	Move 3 spaces	Move 3 spaces
7 + 1	7 + 2	7 + 3
Move 4 spaces	Move 4 spaces	Move 4 spaces
7 + 4	7 + 5	7 + 6
Move 4 spaces	Move 4 spaces	Move 4 spaces
7 + 7	8 + 2	8 + 3
Move 4 spaces	Move 4 spaces	Move 4 spaces
8 + 4	8 + 5	8 + 6
Move 5 spaces	Move 5 spaces	Move 5 spaces
8 + 7	9 + 2	9 + 3
Move 5 spaces	Move 5 spaces	Move 5 spaces
9 + 4	9 + 5	9 + 6
Move 5 spaces	Move 5 spaces	Move 5 spaces

Addition Card	Addition Card	Addition Card
Addition Card	Addition Card	Addition Card
Addition Card	Addition Card	Addition Card
Addition Card	Addition Card	Addition Card
Addition Card	Addition Card	Addition Card
Addition Card	Addition Card	Addition Card
Addition Card	Addition Card	Addition Card

Let's Count to 20

Use the stickers to fill in the missing numbers.

1	2	3	4	5
6	7	8	9	10
11	12	13	14	15
16	17	18	19	20

Use the stickers to fill in the missing numbers.

1	2	3	4	5
6	7	8	9	10
11	12	13	14	15
16	17	18	19	20

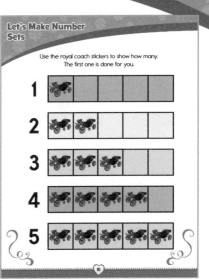

Let's Make Number Sets

Use the royal coach stickers to show how many. The first one is done for you.

1
2
3
4
5

Let's Make Number Bonds to 10

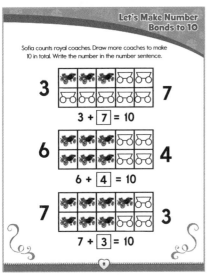

Sofia counts royal coaches. Draw more coaches to make 10 in total. Write the number in the number sentence.

3 ... 7
3 + 7 = 10

6 ... 4
6 + 4 = 10

7 ... 3
7 + 3 = 10

Let's Show Different Ways to Make Numbers

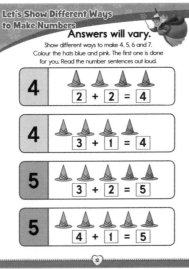

Answers will vary.

Show different ways to make 4, 5, 6 and 7. Colour the hats blue and pink. The first one is done for you. Read the number sentences out loud.

4   2 + 2 = 4
4   3 + 1 = 4
5   3 + 2 = 5
5   4 + 1 = 5

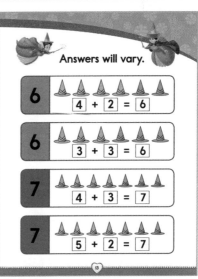

Answers will vary.

6   4 + 2 = 6
6   3 + 3 = 6
7   4 + 3 = 7
7   5 + 2 = 7

Let's Show Different Ways to Make Numbers

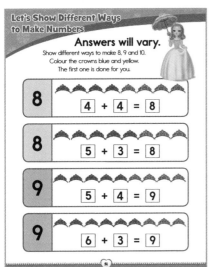

Answers will vary.

Show different ways to make 8, 9 and 10. Colour the crowns blue and yellow. The first one is done for you.

8   4 + 4 = 8
8   5 + 3 = 8
9   5 + 4 = 9
9   6 + 3 = 9

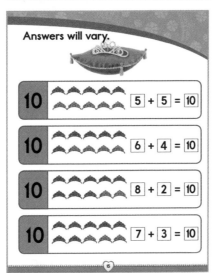

Answers will vary.

10   5 + 5 = 10
10   6 + 4 = 10
10   8 + 2 = 10
10   7 + 3 = 10

Let's Find the Total

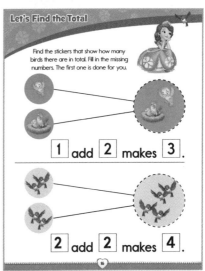

Find the stickers that show how many birds there are in total. Fill in the missing numbers. The first one is done for you.

1 add 2 makes 3.

2 add 2 makes 4.

Answers

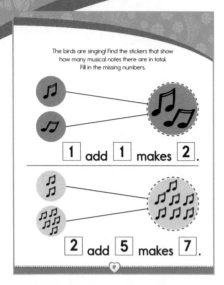

The birds are singing! Find the stickers that show how many musical notes there are in total. Fill in the missing numbers.

1 add 1 makes 2.

2 add 5 makes 7.

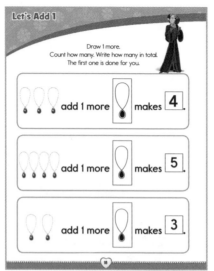

17

Let's Add 1

Draw 1 more.
Count how many. Write how many in total.
The first one is done for you.

add 1 more makes 4.

add 1 more makes 5.

add 1 more makes 3.

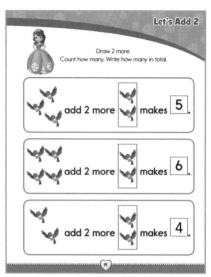

Let's Add 2

Draw 2 more.
Count how many. Write how many in total.

add 2 more makes 5.

add 2 more makes 6.

add 2 more makes 4.

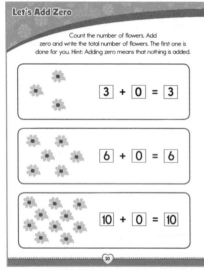

Let's Add Zero

Count the number of flowers. Add zero and write the total number of flowers. The first one is done for you. Hint: Adding zero means that nothing is added.

3 + 0 = 3

6 + 0 = 6

10 + 0 = 10

Let's Solve a Story Problem

Help Sofia compete in the Flying Horseshoe Toss!

First Sofia throws 5 horseshoes.

Then Sofia throws 8 horseshoes.

How many horseshoes has Sofia thrown in total?

Write the number sentence.

5 + 8 = 13

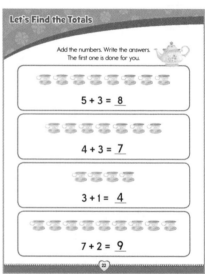

Let's Find the Totals

Add the numbers. Write the answers.
The first one is done for you.

5 + 3 = 8

4 + 3 = 7

3 + 1 = 4

7 + 2 = 9

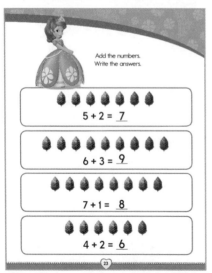

Add the numbers.
Write the answers.

5 + 2 = 7

6 + 3 = 9

7 + 1 = 8

4 + 2 = 6

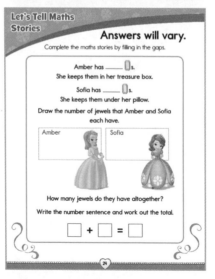

Let's Tell Maths Stories

Answers will vary.

Complete the maths stories by filling in the gaps.

Amber has ____ s.
She keeps them in her treasure box.

Sofia has ____ s.
She keeps them under her pillow.

Draw the number of jewels that Amber and Sofia each have.

Amber	Sofia

How many jewels do they have altogether?

Write the number sentence and work out the total.

☐ + ☐ = ☐

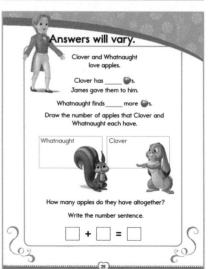

24

Answers will vary.

Clover and Whatnaught love apples.

Clover has ____ s.
James gave them to him.

Whatnaught finds ____ more s.

Draw the number of apples that Clover and Whatnaught each have.

Whatnaught	Clover

How many apples do they have altogether?

Write the number sentence.

☐ + ☐ = ☐

Let's Make Doubles

Add the numbers to double them.
Write the answers.

1 + 1 = __2__

2 + 2 = __4__

3 + 3 = __6__

4 + 4 = __8__

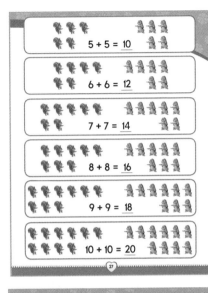

5 + 5 = __10__

6 + 6 = __12__

7 + 7 = __14__

8 + 8 = __16__

9 + 9 = __18__

10 + 10 = __20__

Let's Write Number Sentences

Sofia borrows books from the library.
Write the number sentence shown by the two groups.
Find and write the total. The first one is done for you.

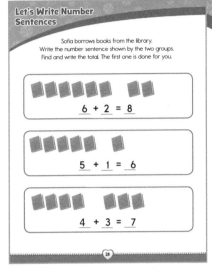

__6__ + __2__ = __8__

__5__ + __1__ = __6__

__4__ + __3__ = __7__

James picks apples from the orchard. Write the number sentence shown by the two groups. Find and write the total.

__8__ + __1__ = __9__

__7__ + __2__ = __9__

__9__ + __1__ = __10__

Let's Find the Totals

Add the numbers and write the answers.
Colour the boxes purple
if the answer is 4 or 8.
The first one is done for you.

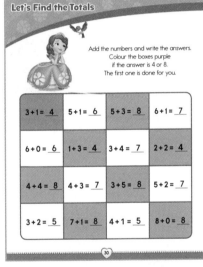

3 + 1 = __4__	5 + 1 = __6__	5 + 3 = __8__	6 + 1 = __7__
6 + 0 = __6__	1 + 3 = __4__	3 + 4 = __7__	2 + 2 = __4__
4 + 4 = __8__	4 + 3 = __7__	3 + 5 = __8__	5 + 2 = __7__
3 + 2 = __5__	7 + 1 = __8__	4 + 1 = __5__	8 + 0 = __8__

Let's Match the Answer

Add the numbers. Write the totals.
Cross out the characters that match the totals.
The last one left is the winner!

| 4 + 3 = __7__ | 3 + 1 = __4__ | 7 + 2 = __9__ |
| 6 + 4 = __10__ | 3 + 2 = __5__ | 5 + 3 = __8__ |

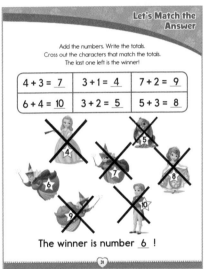

The winner is number __6__ !

Speed Challenge

Solve the calculations.
Record your time and the number of correct answers.
On your marks, get set, go!

1 + 1 = __2__	6 + 3 = __9__	2 + 1 = __3__	5 + 3 = __8__
2 + 2 = __4__	3 + 3 = __6__	8 + 0 = __8__	3 + 2 = __5__
4 + 2 = __6__	5 + 2 = __7__	5 + 1 = __6__	6 + 1 = __7__
9 + 1 = __10__	6 + 2 = __8__	7 + 1 = __8__	8 + 2 = __10__
4 + 3 = __7__	5 + 5 = __10__		Time to Complete: _____ Total Answers: _____ Total Correct: _____

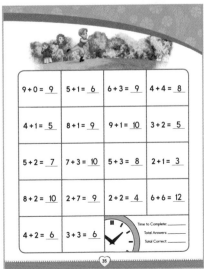

9 + 0 = __9__	5 + 1 = __6__	6 + 3 = __9__	4 + 4 = __8__
4 + 1 = __5__	8 + 1 = __9__	9 + 1 = __10__	3 + 2 = __5__
5 + 2 = __7__	7 + 3 = __10__	5 + 3 = __8__	2 + 1 = __3__
8 + 2 = __10__	2 + 7 = __9__	2 + 2 = __4__	6 + 6 = __12__
4 + 2 = __6__	3 + 3 = __6__		Time to Complete: _____ Total Answers: _____ Total Correct: _____

Let's Count

Jewels sparkle and shine! Count the jewels.
Write the total. The first one is done for you.

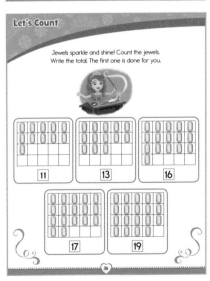

11

13

16

17

19

Answers

Count the teacups. Write the total.

12	**14**	**15**
18	**20**	

Let's Show Ways to Make 5

Look at the flowers.
Use dots to show different ways 5 flowers can go in 2 vases.
The first one is done for you.

Vase 1	Vase 2	Total
● ● ●	● ●	5
● ● ● ●	●	5
● ●	● ● ●	5
●	● ● ● ●	5

Let's Show Ways to Make 9

Amber has tapestries.
Use dots to show different ways 9 tapestries can go in 2 rooms.
The first one is done for you.

Room 1	Room 2	Total
● ● ● ● ● ● ● ●	●	9
● ● ● ● ● ●	● ● ●	9
● ● ● ● ●	● ● ● ●	9
● ● ●	● ● ● ● ● ●	9

Let's Find Totals to 20

Find the totals by counting on from the larger number. Write the answer.

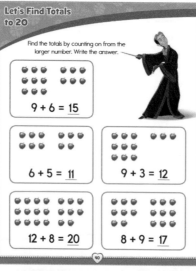

9 + 6 = <u>15</u>

6 + 5 = <u>11</u>   9 + 3 = <u>12</u>

12 + 8 = <u>20</u>   8 + 9 = <u>17</u>

14 + 5 = <u>19</u>

9 + 9 = <u>18</u>   9 + 4 = <u>13</u>

7 + 7 = <u>14</u>   10 + 6 = <u>16</u>

Count On With a Number Line

Use the number line. Count on to add.
Write the total. The first one is done for you.

0 1 2 3 4 5 6 7 8 9 10 11 12 13 14 15

9 + 4 = 13

8 + 3 = 11   9 + 3 = 12

7 + 5 = 12

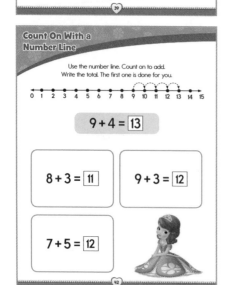

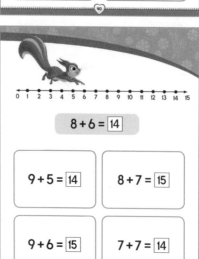

0 1 2 3 4 5 6 7 8 9 10 11 12 13 14 15

8 + 6 = 14

9 + 5 = 14   8 + 7 = 15

9 + 6 = 15   7 + 7 = 14

Let's Write Number Sentences

Write the number sentence.
The first one is done for you.

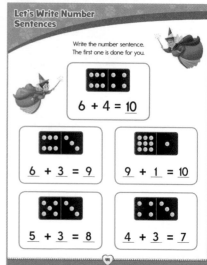

6 + 4 = <u>10</u>

<u>6</u> + <u>3</u> = <u>9</u>   <u>9</u> + <u>1</u> = <u>10</u>

<u>5</u> + <u>3</u> = <u>8</u>   <u>4</u> + <u>3</u> = <u>7</u>

Page 45

Draw the missing dots. Write the number sentence.
The first one is done for you.

7 + <u>2</u> = 9

6 + <u>1</u> = 7

5 + <u>3</u> = 8

<u>5</u> + <u>5</u> = 10

<u>6</u> + <u>4</u> = 10

Let's Add

Add the numbers. Write the totals.
Colour the boxes that have a total of 15.
The first one is done for you.

9 + 6 = 15	7 + 6 = 13	8 + 7 = 15	6 + 5 = 11
8 + 4 = 12	9 + 6 = 15	7 + 4 = 11	8 + 7 = 15
9 + 6 = 15	6 + 4 = 10	8 + 7 = 15	7 + 7 = 14
6 + 3 = 9	6 + 9 = 15	9 + 3 =12	7 + 8 = 15
9 + 6 = 15	8 + 6 = 14	7 + 8 = 15	7 + 5 = 12

Let's Add

Add the numbers. Write the totals.
Colour the boxes that have a total of 18.
The first one is done for you.

11 + 7 = 18	16 + 0 = 16	11 + 9 = 20	7 + 11 = 18
9 + 5 = 14	9 + 9 = 18	12 + 5 = 17	5 + 12 =17
6 + 4 = 10	8 + 7 = 15	8 + 8 = 16	0 + 15 =15
6 + 6 = 12	3 + 9 = 12	13 + 7 = 20	7 + 7 = 14
10 + 9 =19	10 + 8 = 18	18 + 0 = 18	6 + 8 = 14

Let's Look at a Graph

Look at the graph.
Then answer the questions below.

How many 🪺s? <u>6</u>

How many more 🪺s than 🌻s are there? <u>1</u>

How many 🌻s and 🪭s are there in total? <u>10</u>

Let's Solve a Number Puzzle

Add across the grid.
Use your stickers to fill in the missing numbers.

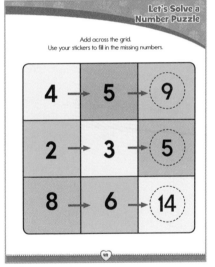

Let's Help the Princesses

Help the princesses get through the maze to the finish line. Colour the squares that have a total of either 11 or 13.

START ↓

	9+1	8+3	
9+3	7+6	7+4	9+4
7+4	9+2		8+6	7+3
8+3	6+6		

FINISH

Let's Match the Answer

Add the numbers. Find the totals.
Cross out the princes and princesses that match the totals.
The person left is the winner!

8 + 5 = <u>13</u>	7 + 7 = <u>14</u>	9 + 3 = <u>12</u>
9 + 2 = <u>11</u>	6 + 3 = <u>9</u>	8 + 7 = <u>15</u>

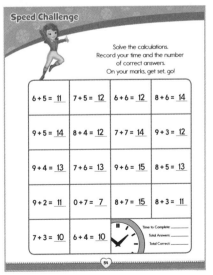

The winner is number <u>10</u> !

Speed Challenge

Solve the calculations.
Record your time and the number of correct answers.
On your marks, get set, go!

6 + 5 = <u>11</u>	7 + 5 = <u>12</u>	6 + 6 = <u>12</u>	8 + 6 = <u>14</u>
9 + 5 = <u>14</u>	8 + 4 = <u>12</u>	7 + 7 = <u>14</u>	9 + 3 = <u>12</u>
9 + 4 = <u>13</u>	7 + 6 = <u>13</u>	9 + 6 = <u>15</u>	8 + 5 = <u>13</u>
9 + 2 = <u>11</u>	0 + 7 = <u>7</u>	8 + 7 = <u>15</u>	8 + 3 = <u>11</u>
7 + 3 = <u>10</u>	6 + 4 = <u>10</u>		

Time to Complete: ____
Total Answers: ____
Total Correct: ____

9 + 6 = <u>15</u>	0 +16 = <u>16</u>	15+4 = <u>19</u>	9 +11 = <u>20</u>
12+4 = <u>16</u>	9 + 9 = <u>18</u>	12 + 5 = <u>17</u>	4 +14 = <u>18</u>
6 + 7 = <u>13</u>	11 + 7 = <u>18</u>	8 + 8 = <u>16</u>	6 +13 = <u>19</u>
15 + 0 = <u>15</u>	13 + 5 = <u>18</u>	6 + 6 = <u>12</u>	7 + 7 = <u>14</u>
10 + 9 = <u>19</u>	12 + 8 = <u>20</u>		

Time to Complete: ____
Total Answers: ____
Total Correct: ____

Here Are All The Things I Can Do!

Put a flower sticker next to each thing that you can do.

I can ...

Count, sequence and write numbers to 20	⬤	Show different ways to make 7	⬤
Work out number bonds to 10	⬤	Show different ways to make 8	⬤
Show different ways to make 4	⬤	Show different ways to make 9	⬤
Show different ways to make 5	⬤	Show different ways to make 10	⬤
Show different ways to make 6	⬤	Count numbers greater than 10	⬤

Find the total of two groups of objects ◯

Solve calculations using addition ◯

Add 1 more ◯

Use a number line to count on ◯

Add 2 more ◯

Use a graph ◯

Find totals to 10 ◯

Solve a number puzzle ◯

Find totals to 20 ◯

Work out doubles for numbers up to 10 ◯

Solve story problems using addition ◯

Add zero to a number ◯

Write story problems using addition ◯

Write number sentences ◯

More Activities to Share with Your Child

How does your child learn?

Research shows that all children benefit from a wide range of learning activities. Here are a few exercises to do together to strengthen your child's understanding of basic addition concepts.

Practise maths at meal times

Snack time is perfect for practising addition concepts. Place two plates on the table. Put two pieces of fruit on each plate. Ask your child to close his or her eyes. Then add an extra piece of fruit to one plate. Ask your child to look and see if they can quickly work out without counting how many items are on each plate now. Ask questions like, 'Which plate has more fruit on it?', 'Which plate has fewer pieces of fruit on it?' or 'How many pieces of fruit did I add?'

Put the pieces of fruit together. Ask, 'How many pieces of fruit are there altogether?', or 'Can you tell me the number sentence that you have made?' Repeat with different quantities and adding different amounts.

Use a calendar to count on

To begin, point to a number on the calendar. Then ask your child to say a number that is one more, two more or three more. Ask them, 'How did you work that out?'

Add with beads

Count and add with colourful beads.

To make the dough beads you need:

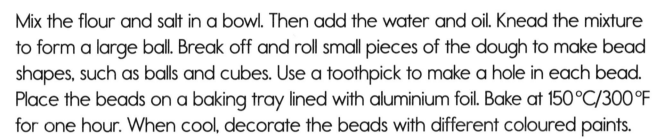

50g flour	50g salt
250ml cold water	30ml cooking oil

Mix the flour and salt in a bowl. Then add the water and oil. Knead the mixture to form a large ball. Break off and roll small pieces of the dough to make bead shapes, such as balls and cubes. Use a toothpick to make a hole in each bead. Place the beads on a baking tray lined with aluminium foil. Bake at 150°C/300°F for one hour. When cool, decorate the beads with different coloured paints.

Make number bracelets with two colours. Decide on a number, such as eight. Then, ask your child to thread two different colours of beads on a piece of string. Work together to see how many different combinations you can make for eight (six and two; seven and one; five and three; four and four).

Count and add with coins

Place a small handful of coins into a bowl. Start with 1ps and 2ps. Ask your child to sort the coins. Work together to calculate the value of different sets of coins. Some children will need help understanding that six 1p coins have the same value as three 2p coins. Introduce other coins as your child's confidence grows. Ask questions like, 'Show me 6p. If I give you 3p more, how much money will you have?' or 'How much money is £6 added to £3?'

More Activities to Share with Your Child

Make a tens frame

Cut two cups off a large egg carton that you have a container that has ten compartments. Use two different colours of buttons or other small objects to count and add. Ask your child to put five objects in the container and then add three more of the other colour. See if your child can work how many objects there are in total without counting them all. Then count the objects together.

Create 'one more' stories

Use the characters from **Sofia the First** to help your child to create 'one more', 'two more' or 'three more' stories. For example, 'Sofia picked four flowers to put in her vase. Then she picked three more. How many flowers did Sofia pick in total?' Use counting objects to illustrate the story.

Provide drawing materials for your child to illustrate the addition stories. Help your child to write the number sentence below their illustration.

How many objects are hidden?

Count out five small objects with your child, such as coins, buttons or beads. Ask your child to close their eyes. Hide three of the objects in your right hand. Ask your child to open their eyes and say how many objects they can still see (two). Say to your child, 'There were five beads. Now you can see two beads. How many beads are hidden in my right hand?'

Encourage them to work out the answer by using their knowledge of pairs of numbers that total five. Then show how many beads were hidden. Ask your child to write down the number sentence that they solved: '2 + 3 = 5.' Repeat this with different numbers, initially up to twelve.

Play addition games

Practise simple addition facts with a pair of dice or some dominoes. Take turns rolling the dice or turning over a domino. Add the two numbers together to find the total. The player with the larger total gets a point or a counter. Decide how many rounds you will have. The player with the most points or counters wins the game.

You could make up different rules to invent your own game.

Add anytime!

You can play number games anywhere that will develop your child's ability to add numbers mentally. For example, in the shops, in the car or walking to school. You could count how many red cars or dogs that you can see. Say a number and ask your child to tell you a number that is 'one more' or 'two more'. Say two or three numbers out loud (for example, three, one and four) and ask your child to tell you the total. Can they make up a number story involving these numbers? Can they tell you some number sentences involving these numbers? For example: '3 + 1 = 4' or '4 + 3 + 1 = 8'.

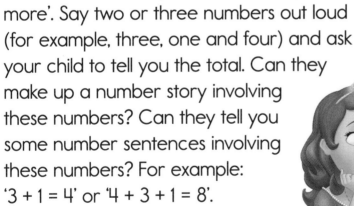

Merryweather has a secret message

Read her message:

1. Solve each problem.
2. Write the total in each ☐.
3. Look at the number key.
4. Write the letter in the ◯ that matches the total.
5. The first problem is done for you.

$7+5=$ **12** ◉

$6+5=$ ☐ ◯,

$3+2=$ ☐ ◯

$5+5=$ ☐ ◯

$4+4=$ ☐ ◯

$8+4=$ ☐ ◯

$6+3=$ ☐ ◯

$8+3=$ ☐ ◯ !

$2+2=$ ☐ ◯

$9+4=$ ☐ ◯

$6+1=$ ☐ ◯

$4+2=$ ☐ ◯

$9+6=$ ☐ ◯

$6+6=$ ☐ ◯

$7+7=$ ☐ ◯ !

Number Key:

4 . . . . . N	8 . . . . . G	12 . . . . . O
5 . . . . . M	9 . . . . S	13 I
6 . . . . . E	10 . . . . Y	14 . . . . B
7 C	11 . . . . H	15 . . . . J

Congratulations!

_____
(Name)

has completed the Disney Learning Workbook:

Adding

Presented on

_____
(Date)

_____
(Parent's Signature)